DISCOVER!

AMERICA'S AMAZING LANDMARKS

THE WASHINGTON MONUMENT

By Marie Roesser

Enslow PUBLISHING

Please visit our website, www.enslow.com. For a free color catalog of all our high-quality books, call toll free 1-800-398-2504 or fax 1-877-980-4454.

Library of Congress Cataloging-in-Publication Data
Names: Roesser, Marie, author.
Title: The Washington Monument / Marie Roesser.
Description: New York : Enslow Publishing, [2026] | Series: America's amazing landmarks | Includes bibliographical references and index.
Identifiers: LCCN 2025000019 (print) | LCCN 2025000020 (ebook) | ISBN 9781978544109 (library binding) | ISBN 9781978544093 (paperback) | ISBN 9781978544116 (ebook)
Subjects: LCSH: Washington Monument (Washington D.C.)–Juvenile literature. | Washington, George, 1732-1799–Monuments–Washington (D.C.)–Juvenile literature. | Washington (D.C.)–Buildings, structures, etc.–Juvenile literature.
Classification: LCC F203.4.W3 R64 2026 (print) | LCC F203.4.W3 (ebook) | DDC 975.3–dc23/eng/20250207
LC record available at https://lccn.loc.gov/2025000019
LC ebook record available at https://lccn.loc.gov/2025000020

Portions of this work were originally authored by Natalie Joseph and published as *Visit the Washington Monument*. All new material this edition authored by Marie Roesser.

Published in 2026 by
Enslow Publishing
2544 Clinton Street2
Buffalo, NY 14224

Cover Designer: Nicholas Switalski
Interior Designer: Rachel Rising
Editor: Therese Shea

Photo credits: Cover, p. 1 ParkerCV/Shutterstock.com; Cover, pp. 1, 3-24 Jeffery Edwards/Shutterstock.com; pp. 1, 5, 9, 11, 15, 17, 19, 21 Oleksandr Poliashenko/Shutterstock.com; p. 5 Peter Hermes Furian/Shutterstock.com; p. 5 S.Borisov/Shutterstock.com; p. 6 https://commons.wikimedia.org/wiki/File:Washington_1772.jpg; p. 7 https://commons.wikimedia.org/wiki/File:Washington_the_soldier.jpg; p. 9 https://commons.wikimedia.org/wiki/File:George_Washington,_1776.jpg; p. 11 https://commons.wikimedia.org/wiki/File:Surrender_of_Lord_Cornwallis.jpg; p. 13 https://commons.wikimedia.org/wiki/File:Scene_at_the_Signing_of_the_Constitution_of_the_United_States.jpg; p. 14 Sachin Graphics/Shutterstock.com; p. 15 https://commons.wikimedia.org/wiki/File:Gilbert_Stuart_-_George_Washington_(Lansdowne_Portrait)_-_Google_Art_Project.jpg; p. 17 https://commons.wikimedia.org/wiki/File:Washington_Monument_circa_1860_-_Brady-Handy.jpg; p. 18 PeskyMonkey/Shutterstock.com; p. 19 eurobanks/Shutterstock.com; p. 21 PinkCuke/Shutterstock.com.

Printed in the United States of America

CPSIA compliance information: Batch #CSENS26: For further information contact Enslow Publishing, at 1-800-398-2504.

CONTENTS

BOLDFACE WORDS APPEAR IN THE GLOSSARY.

MORE THAN A PRESIDENT

George Washington was more than a president. He was a general who helped win the **American Revolution** and a **Founding Father** of the nation. His strong leadership is why he became the first U.S. president. The Washington Monument honors this famous American.

THE WASHINGTON MONUMENT IS LOCATED IN WASHINGTON, D.C.

YOUNG WASHINGTON

Washington was born in the Virginia **colony** on February 22, 1732. He was a **surveyor** for his first job. Then he joined the Virginia **militia**. He fought bravely for the British during the French and Indian War (1754–1763).

Battle of the Monongahela, July 9, 1755
George Washington

A FIGHT FOR RIGHTS

After the French and Indian War, Great Britain passed laws and taxes that made many colonists unhappy. Washington believed the British were taking away colonists' rights. He became a Virginia **representative** at the First and Second **Continental Congress**. The representatives voted for independence, or freedom.

IN 1775, THE SECOND CONTINENTAL CONGRESS CHOSE WASHINGTON AS COMMANDER IN CHIEF OF THE COLONIAL ARMY.

WASHINGTON'S ARMY

The colonial army, called the Continental army, was made up of mostly untrained soldiers. The Americans had little money to pay their soldiers. Supplies were few. But the soldiers respected Washington. He was an **inspiring** leader who led them to win the war.

THE LAST MAJOR BATTLE OF THE AMERICAN REVOLUTION WAS AT YORKTOWN, VIRGINIA, IN SEPTEMBER 1781. WASHINGTON'S ARMY WON.

THE FIRST ELECTION

In 1787, Washington was named the president of the Constitutional Convention. This special meeting created the U.S. Constitution, the highest law in the nation. It said the country would have three branches of government. One branch would be led by a president. In 1789, George Washington was elected the first U.S. president.

Constitutional Convention of 1787
George Washington

WASHINGTON, D.C.

In 1790, Washington chose the site for the building of the nation's new capital. The capital city was named Washington in his honor in 1791. The area around it was named the **District** of Columbia (D.C.) for Christopher Columbus.

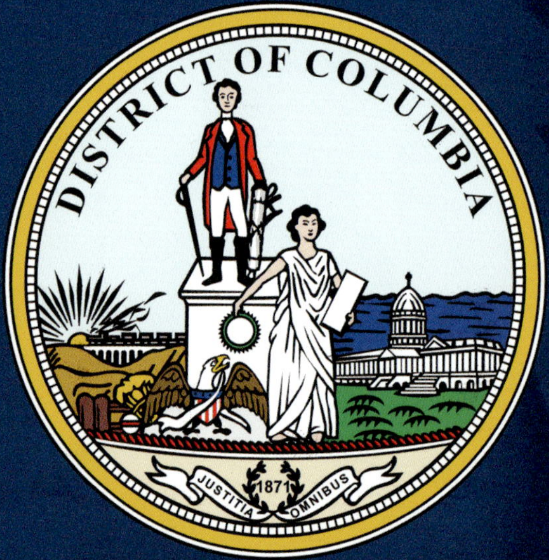

AFTER HIS PRESIDENCY, WASHINGTON RETURNED TO HIS HOME, MOUNT VERNON, IN 1797.

THE MAKING OF THE MONUMENT

George Washington died December 14, 1799. A plan for a monument to him was approved in 1836. **Architect** Robert Mills designed, or planned, it. The first stone was laid July 4, 1848. Countries, states, and groups gave stones to build the monument. The slow work was completed in 1884.

WORK ON THE MONUMENT STOPPED DURING THE AMERICAN CIVIL WAR, A WAR FOUGHT BETWEEN THE STATES FROM 1861 TO 1865.

MONUMENT MEASUREMENTS

The Washington Monument stands 554 feet 7 inches (169 m) tall. It's the tallest stone structure and obelisk in the world. The walls are covered with white marble. The monument is hollow. The inside walls are stones with designs or writing on them.

AN OBELISK IS A COLUMN OF STONE WITH A SQUARE BASE, SIDES THAT SLOPE IN, AND A PYRAMID ON TOP.

VISIT THE MONUMENT

The Washington Monument is located on the **National Mall** and is surrounded by 50 flags, which represent the 50 U.S. states. The National Park Service cares for the monument. Park rangers answer visitors' questions about it. If you go to Washington, D.C., visit the Washington Monument!

AN ELEVATOR TAKES PEOPLE TO THE TOP OF THE WASHINGTON MONUMENT!

GLOSSARY

architect: A person who designs buildings.

American Revolution: The war in which the colonies won their freedom from England.

colony: A piece of land under the control of another country.

Continental Congress: A meeting of colonial representatives before, during, and after the American Revolution.

district: An area with a special feature or government.

Founding Father: A leader in the founding of the United States.

inspiring: Causing someone to want to do something.

militia: A group of citizens who organize like soldiers to protect themselves.

National Mall: A park with many monuments in Washington, D.C., the capital city of the United States.

representative: A member of a decision-making body who acts for others.

surveyor: One whose job is to measure land areas.

FOR MORE INFORMATION

Books

Gilmore, Frederic. *The Washington Monument: A Tribute to a Man, a Monument for a Nation*. Mankato, MN: The Child's World, 2024.

Knopp, Ezra E. *Myths and Facts About George Washington*. Buffalo, NY: PowerKids Press, 2024.

Websites

George Washington
kids.nationalgeographic.com/history/article/george-washington
Read more about the president's life.

Washington Monument
www.nps.gov/wamo/index.htm
Plan your visit to this record-breaking monument.

Publisher's note to educators and parents: Our editors have carefully reviewed these websites to ensure that they are suitable for students. Many websites change frequently, however, and we cannot guarantee that a site's future contents will continue to meet our high standards of quality and educational value. Be advised that students should be closely supervised whenever they access the internet.

INDEX